The EVOLUTION OF HOCKEY

F

The EVOLUTION OF HOCKEY

Dave Elston

Foreword by Steve Dryden

M&S

Canadian Cataloguing in Publication Data

Elston, Dave, 1958-
The evolution of hockey

ISBN 0-7710-3054-1

1. Hockey – Caricatures and cartoons. 2. Canadian with humor,
Pictorial. I. Title.

NC1449.E48A4 1999   741.5'971   C99-931852-7

We acknowledge the financial support of the Government of Canada
through the Book Publishing Industry Development Program for
our publishing activities. We further acknowledge the support of the
Canada Council for the Arts and the Ontario Arts Council for our
publishing program.

Canadä

Designed by Terri-Anne Fong
Typeset in Caslon by M&S, Toronto

Printed and bound in Canada

McClelland & Stewart Inc.
The Canadian Publishers
481 University Avenue
Toronto, Ontario
M5G 2E9

1 2 3 4 5   03 02 01 00 99

FOREWORD

Dave Elston is the ultimate poster boy for college dropouts. Not only could he represent the disillusioned, the discouraged, and the displaced, but he could design and illustrate the poster for them. Elston dropped out of art school – perhaps before he was asked to leave – to embark on a unique career in journalism. He is the only full-time sports cartoonist in Canada and one of only a handful in North America, working at the *Calgary Sun* since 1980. The Edmonton native lasted one week into his third year at the Alberta College of Art before deciding to take the hint. His work was dismissed as "cartoony." That didn't appeal to art school sensibilities. "There was no such thing as a good cartoon," Elston says. "The only good cartoon was a dead cartoon." He was nearing a career crossroads when a professor sniffed, "One of these days you're going to have to get serious." Elston did. He got serious about cartooning, signing up as a freelancer with the *Sun* and taking on the sports establishment, armed only with a sledgehammer sense of humour and a quill pen. Nineteen years later, he is in a class by himself – in part, he points out, because there is no one else in his class. Elston says "lack of competition" is one of the secrets to his success. A more significant reason is his extraordinary talent for packing single panel cartoons full of humour and humanity. Elston is an all-round threat in the sports world, choosing his subjects from rodeo to road racing to running. But it's in hockey that Elston has made his biggest impact. Since joining *The Hockey News* in 1985, he has become hockey's premier satirist, and is so admired that even his victims are more likely to smile than sling mud in response. Nobody has been lampooned more often than Theoren Fleury, a convenient target because Fleury played nearly eleven seasons in Calgary. The feisty Fleury, generously listed as five-foot-six, was not always among Elston's fans, but joined the crowd when the two met: "A mutual friend introduced us and I think he was a little taken aback by my size," Elston says. "He likes to say he towers over me." Elston is five-foot-three. His success establishes once and for all that size doesn't matter – in cartooning, anyway, where Elston has grown into a giant figure.

Steve Dryden
Editor-in-Chief
The Hockey News

THE ICE AGE

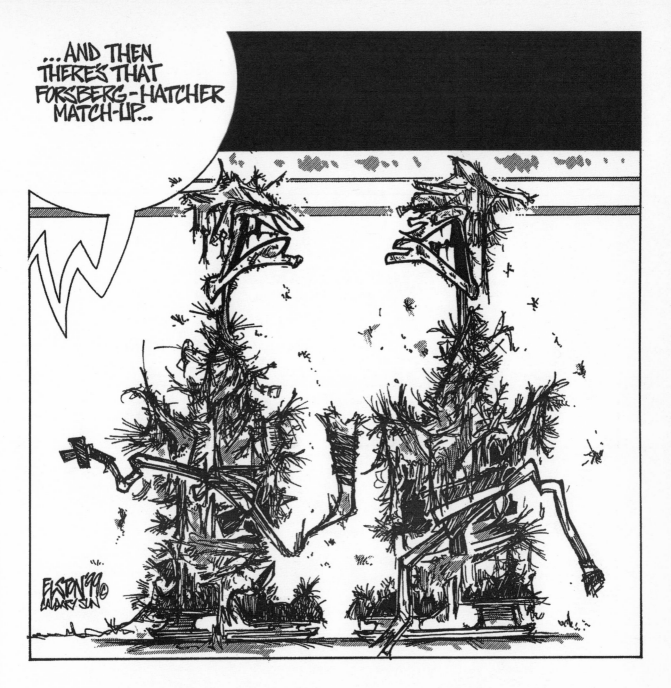

Peter Forsberg of the Colorado Avalanche and Derian Hatcher
of the Dallas Stars went toe-to-toe in the 1999 Stanley Cup semifinals.

The Dallas Stars defeated the Buffalo Sabres
in the 1999 Stanley Cup final in six games.

The Dallas Stars' Stanley Cup celebrations were somewhat tainted because critics felt that Brett Hull's overtime goal to win the series had not been reviewed properly.

Buffalo Sabres goalie Dominik Hasek stonewalled
the second-seeded Ottawa Senators in a four-game sweep
en route to an appearance in the 1999 Stanley Cup final.

Buffalo Sabres goalie Dominik Hasek sometimes wore
a special girdle during the 1999 playoffs to protect a groin injury.

The Pittsburgh Penguins filed for bankruptcy
during the 1998-99 season after running into money problems.

Mike Ilitch, owner of the Detroit Red Wings and Little Caesars Pizza, acquired Wendel Clark, Ulf Samuelsson, and Bill Ranford late in the 1998-99 season to help the Wings in their ultimately unsuccessful playoff run.

After sitting out most of the 1997-98 season, Sergei Fedorov inked
a six-year, $38-million deal that included a $14-million signing bonus.

WEEKEND AT VERNIE'S

Goalie Mike Vernon won the Conn Smythe Trophy, as playoff MVP,
after the Detroit Red Wings won the Stanley Cup in 1997.

The Washington Capitals annually
lead the NHL in man-games lost to injury.

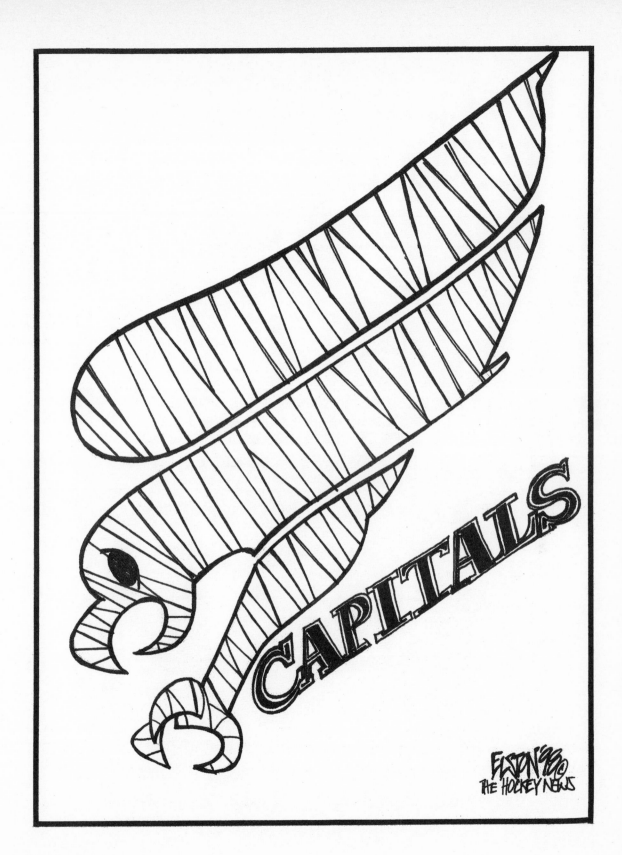

For the 1998-99 season, Chicago Blackhawks GM Bob Murray
made the mistake of hiring a novice coach, Dirk Graham.
Murray fired Graham after fifty-nine games, saying he would
never put anybody in that position again.

THE BLACKHAWKS

THEN

NOW

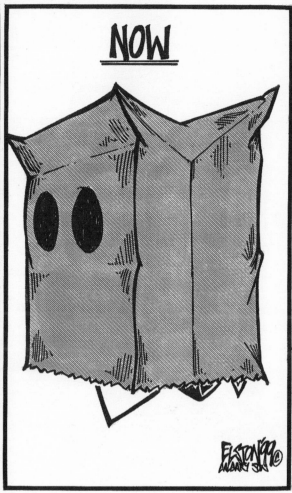

The Chicago Blackhawks missed the playoffs
in back-to-back seasons (1997-98 and 1998-99)
for the first time in forty-one years.

OFFICIAL PASTIME OF THE HOCKEY GODS

The New York Islanders won four straight Stanley Cups
during the early 1980s. By the end of the 1990s, the Isles, after years of weak teams
and suspect management, had become a league embarrassment.

The 1997-98 Tampa Bay Lightning
were one of the worst scoring teams in NHL history.

The woeful Hartford Whalers, who had only
three winning seasons in their eighteen years as an NHL club,
headed south in 1997 to Carolina.

The Carolina Hurricanes had the NHL's
worst attendance in the two seasons they played
at the Greensboro Coliseum.

The Carolina Hurricanes reduced seating capacity at the
Greensboro Coliseum to eliminate gaping sections of empty seats.

Colorado swept Florida in four games to win
the 1996 Stanley Cup, outscoring the Panthers 15-4.

A VANCOUVER CANUCKS UPDATE

The Vancouver Canucks' regular-season point totals dropped
three straight seasons after last making the playoffs in 1995-96.

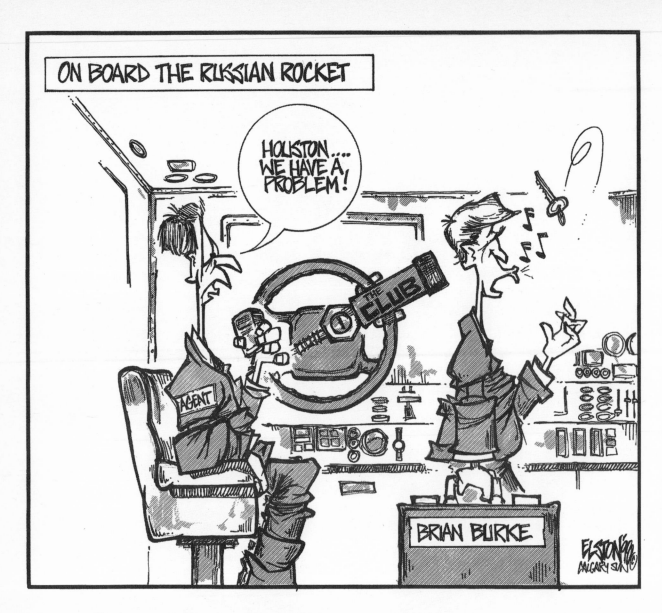

Feeling underpaid and underappreciated by the Vancouver Canucks,
Russian superstar Pavel Bure refused to report
for the 1998-99 season. GM Brian Burke let him sit until January
when he finally traded him to the Florida Panthers.

THE NEW-LOOK CANUCKS

Vancouver Canucks GM Brian Burke and coach Mike Keenan
butted heads several times in their short tenure together before
Burke fired Keenan the day after the 1999 All-Star Game.

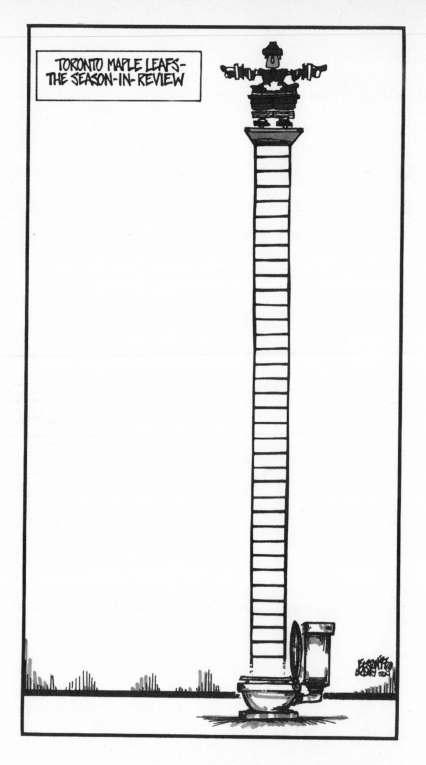

After a string of four straight playoff appearances,
the Toronto Maple Leafs missed the post-season in 1996-97.

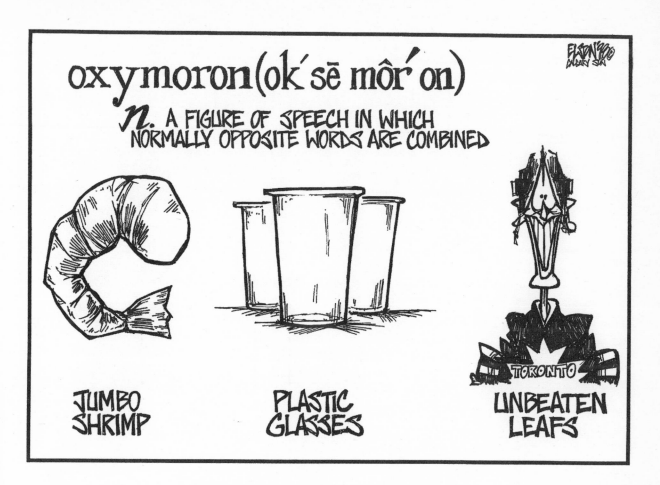

The usually inept Toronto Maple Leafs
started 1998-99 with three straight victories.

The Calgary Flames' power play went from one of the NHL's best
in 1996-97 to one of the worst the following season.

Having missed the playoffs only once since their Stanley Cup victory in 1989, the Calgary Flames finished 1996-1997 with their worst record since their inaugural season in Atlanta twenty-four years earlier.

The Edmonton Oilers and Calgary Flames had many intense
playoff battles during the 1980s. Since 1990,
they have made the playoffs in the same season only once, in 1991.

Montreal, Winnipeg, Vancouver, Calgary, and Toronto
all made the 1996 playoffs, but each team was bounced in the
first round, guaranteeing a U.S.–based Stanley Cup winner.

The Winnipeg Jets headed for the desert
when they became the Phoenix Coyotes in 1996-97.

SURVIVAL OF THE FITTEST

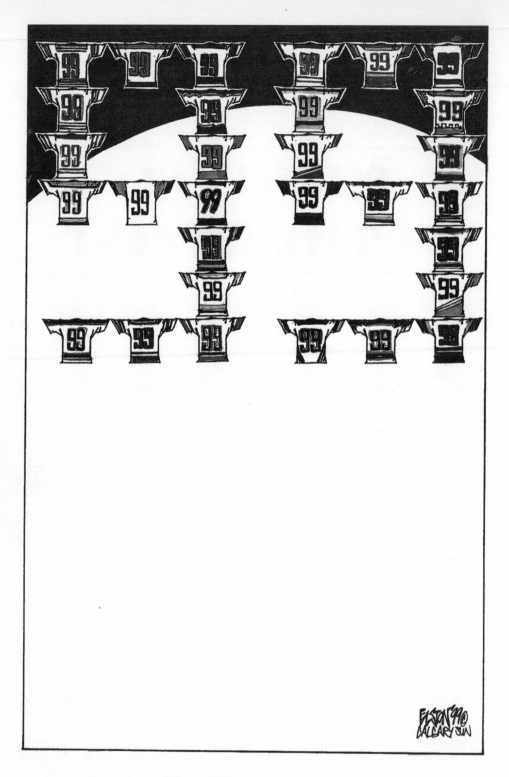

The NHL retires No. 99.

BITTEN BY THE Y2K BUG, THE NHL'S SCORING STATS ARE ENTIRELY DELETED
WHADDAYA MEAN I HAVE TO START OVER??
GRETZKY
ELSTON'99©

Jaromir Jagr of the Pittsburgh Penguins
issues a military salute after every goal he scores.

VIEW FROM THE
MIKE RICCI-CAM

Despite another strong regular season, Eric Lindros
and the Philadelphia Flyers were dumped in the first round
of the 1998 playoffs by the underdog Buffalo Sabres.

Gordie Howe laced up for the Detroit Vipers
of the International Hockey League for one game in 1997 so he
could say that he played pro hockey in six different decades.

THE PUPPA SCOOPER

Goalie Daren Puppa has been one of the few bright spots
for the Tampa Bay Lightning since they entered the NHL in 1992-93.

After representing Canada at the 1996 World Cup, Rob Blake
returned to a Los Angeles Kings squad that hadn't made
the playoffs since their appearance in the Stanley Cup final in 1993.

HOCKEY NIGHTMARE #837
CRAIG LUDWIG DISCOVERS THAT....
...OVER TIME, HIS LEGS HAVE BECOME THE SAME SIZE AS HIS SHINPADS.
STARS
ELSTON '98 © CALGARY SUN

Detroit Red Wings centre Kris Draper suffered major facial injuries
when Colorado Avalanche right winger Claude Lemieux
checked him from behind in the 1996 Western Conference final.

San Jose Sharks defenceman Bryan Marchment
has been suspended several times for checking players knee-first.

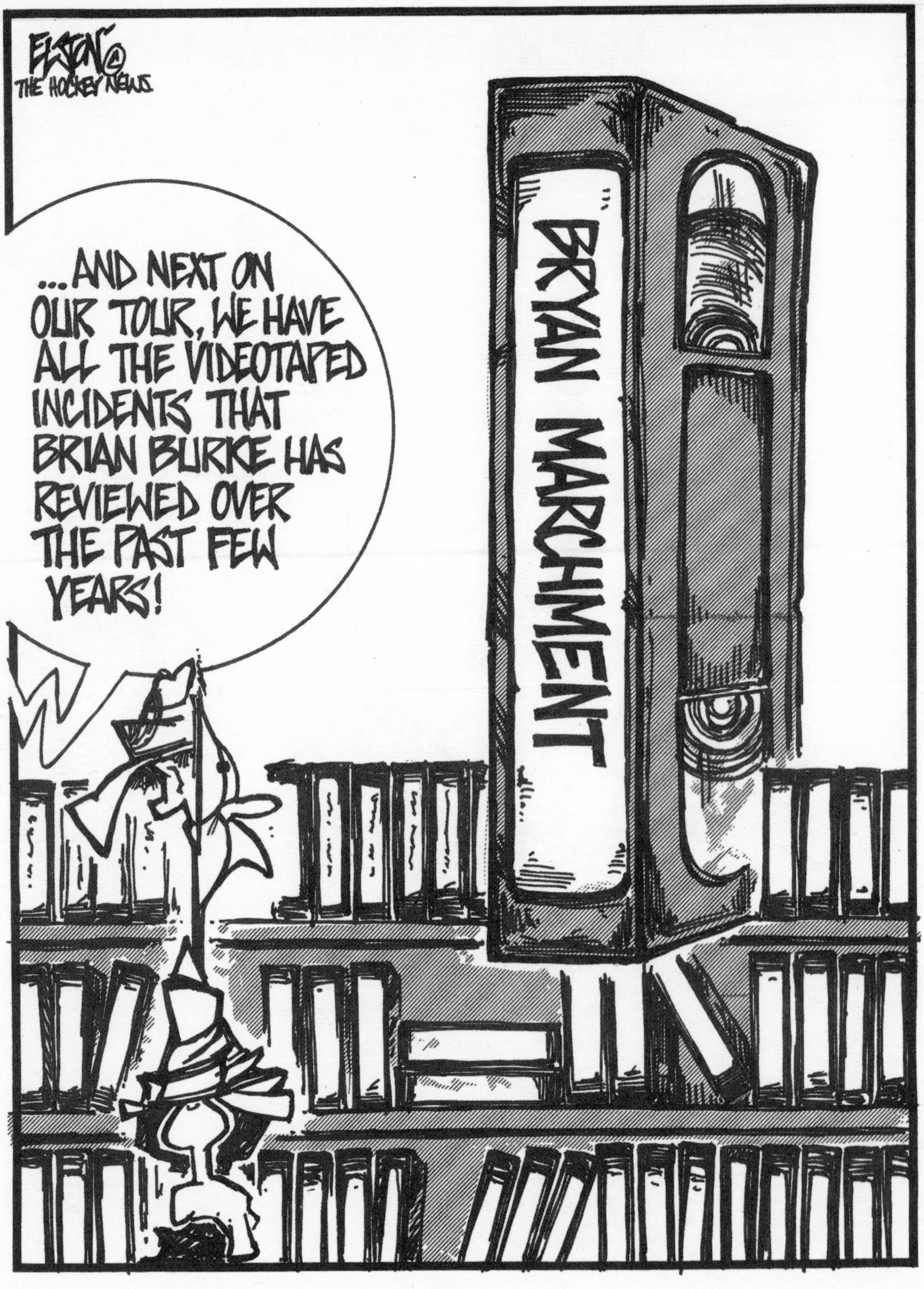
ELSTON © THE HOCKEY NEWS
...AND NEXT ON OUR TOUR, WE HAVE ALL THE VIDEOTAPED INCIDENTS THAT BRIAN BURKE HAS REVIEWED OVER THE PAST FEW YEARS!
BRYAN MARCHMENT

THE OFFICIAL
DOUG GILMOUR TOOTHBRUSH

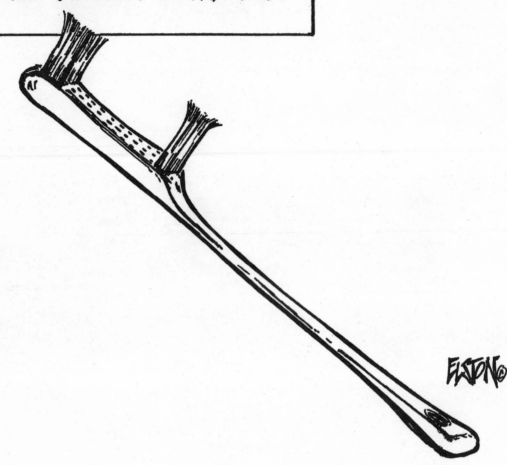

Contrary to what most would consider the sane
alternative – a trade out of Toronto – Doug Gilmour insisted he wanted
to remain a Maple Leaf before his 1997 trade to New Jersey.

Buffalo Sabres GM John Muckler and coach Ted Nolan
were mortal enemies by the end of the 1996-97 season.
Neither survived the off-season with the team.

The scoreboard at the Marine Midland Arena,
home of the Buffalo Sabres, crashed to the ice in November 1996.

During the 1996-1997 season, Buffalo Sabres captain Pat Lafontaine suffered a serious concussion that put him out for the rest of the season. The Sabres, feeling he hadn't fully recovered, later traded him to the New York Rangers.

KERRY FRASER

Disgraced hockey czar Alan Eagleson

was found guilty of fraud and theft charges in 1999.

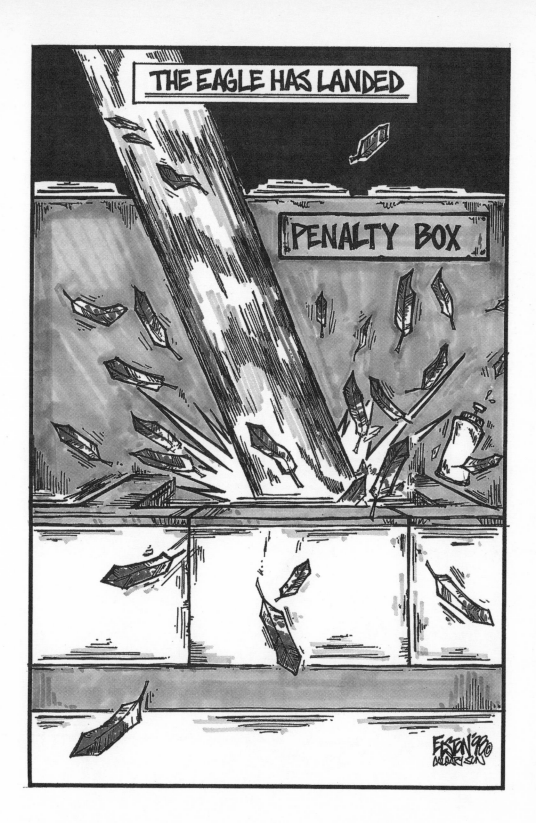

OFFICIAL WHISTLE OF THE NHL COACHING FRATERNITY

Division rivals New York Rangers, Tampa Bay Lightning,
Philadelphia Flyers, Florida Panthers, and New York Islanders
all changed coaches during the 1997-1998 season.

Philadelphia Flyers coach Roger Neilson was suspended two games and fined $10,000 in 1999 for throwing a stick onto the ice in protest of an official's call.

Neil Smith, the GM of the New York Rangers,
went on the biggest spending spree in NHL history when he signed
Theoren Fleury and five others after the 1998-99 season.

Even though coach Wayne Cashman led the
Philadelphia Flyers to a 32-20-9 record, he was fired in favour
of Roger Neilson late in the 1997-98 season.

The Detroit Red Wings defeated Mike Keenan's
St. Louis Blues in the 1996 Stanley Cup conference semifinals.

Former Montreal Canadiens goalie Ken Dryden
took over as Toronto Maple Leafs president and GM in 1997.

Restricted free agent Doug Weight did not report
to the Edmonton Oilers' 1998-99 training camp in an effort to squeeze
more money out of GM Glen Sather.

High-priced talent was moved near the 1997 trade deadline.

Cam Neely's career came to a premature end
in 1996 due to chronic hip problems.

THE LAW
OF THE JUNGLE

ALEXANDER GRAHAM BELL INVENTS THE TELEPHONE
MR. WATSON, COME HERE....
... YOU'VE BEEN TRADED!

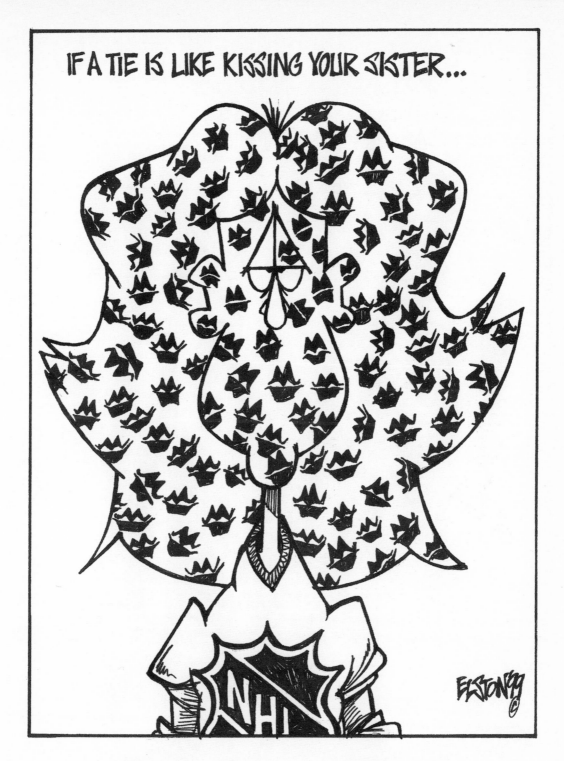

IF A TIE IS LIKE KISSING YOUR SISTER...

During the 1998-99 season, 162 NHL games
ended in a tie, a concern for the league.

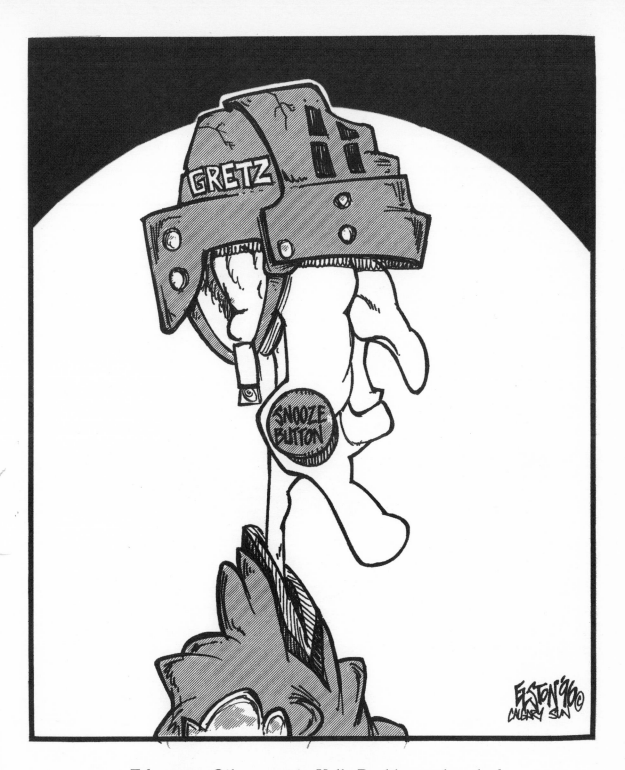

Edmonton Oilers captain Kelly Buchberger knocked
Wayne Gretzky cold for several minutes
in one of No. 99's first games with the St. Louis Blues.

Defenceman Dave Manson has a well-earned reputation
for losing it in the heat of battle.

Dave Manson had his voice box damaged when Sergio Momesso punched him in the throat during a scuffle in 1991.

Tie Domi of the Toronto Maple Leafs was suspended eight games in 1995 for suckerpunching Ulf Samuelsson of the New York Rangers.

ROCKY AND BULLWINKLE

Flames enforcer Rocky Thompson became a fan favourite
in Calgary for his fighting exploits when he was called up in 1998.

NHL all-star games are notorious no-hit affairs.

The NHL was seen to be kowtowing to the FOX television network
during their five-year relationship.

Detroit's four-game sweep over Washington in the 1998 Stanley Cup final didn't capture the imagination of viewers. Television ratings dipped thirty-three per cent from the previous year's final.

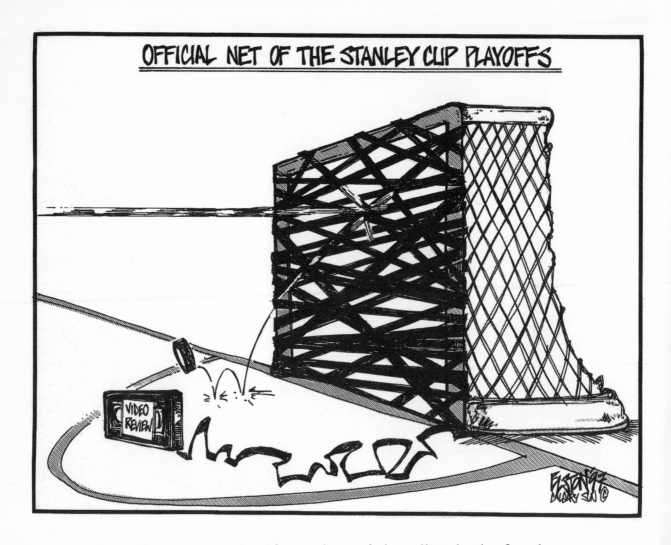

Controversy over video replay and the calling back of goals
has plagued the NHL since the league adopted replay in 1991-92.

TEEMU WAS ON THE VERGE OF ACCEPTING THE AWARD FOR MOST GOALS SCORED IN THE REGULAR SEASON WHEN SUDDENLY, THE REFEREE DECIDED TO GO UPSTAIRS.

THE EXPANDING NHL

← THE TALENT LEVEL

HAMILTON MAKES ITS BID FOR AN NHL EXPANSION FRANCHISE
HELL
OKAY! BRING IN THE SNOWBALL!!

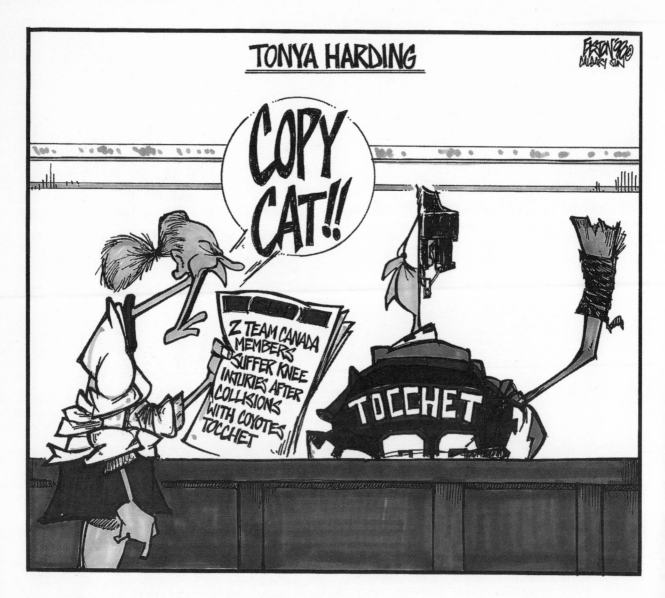

Trevor Linden and Steve Yzerman had their Olympic dreams flash before their eyes after collisions with Rick Tocchet prior to the 1998 Winter Games.

Team Canada GM Bob Clarke was roundly criticized
for not selecting Mark Messier to the 1998 Winter Olympics roster.

Paul Kariya missed the 1998 Winter Olympics, as well as the rest
of the 1997-1998 season, after Gary Suter cross-checked him in the jaw.

Seeking to win their first medal since the "Miracle on Ice" in 1980,
the Americans not only bombed at the 1998 Winter Games,
but several players also ransacked their rooms in the Olympic village.